PRAISE FOR SHERNA SPENCER

"Spencer's book is a jolt of inspiration."
— Derek "Laddie" Kong, Yardi Books

"...reverberates with an energy and the effervescent joy of being human. Reading these poems is a comforting and fulfilling experience, where everyone can find a few familiar pastures."
— Rita Fidler Dorn, Poet, professor of English at Florida International University, Miami, FL, past president of South Florida Writers Association

"...poems are good. Cleverly written."
— Dr. Sheryl A. Ferguson, Licensed Psychologist
The Assessment, Counseling & Development Center

Also by Sherna Spencer

Musing Aloud, Allowed, a collection of 40 funny, inspiring and thought provoking poems about life and current events.

Three Echoes Dancing

Poetry celebrating each stage of our lives

By Sherna Spencer

Three Echoes Dancing. Copyright ©2016, by Sherna G. Spencer.
Cover art by: Helen Wood. Book design by: John Vincent Palozzi

All rights reserved. Except as permitted under the U.S. Copyright Act of 1976, no part of this publication may be reproduced, distributed, or transmitted in any form or by any means, or stored in a database or retrieval system, without the prior written permission of the publisher.

>Published by JALOUSIE
>An imprint of SGS Publishing, LLC
>4500 W. Oakland Park Boulevard, Ste 103
>Fort Lauderdale, FL 33313
>www.lookitsthebook.com

Three Echoes Dancing is a work of fiction. Names, characters, places, and incidents are the product of the author's imagination or are used fictionally. Any resemblance to actual events, locales, or persons, living or dead, is coincidental.

Publisher's Cataloging-in-Publication data

Spencer, Sherna G
>Three Echoes Dancing: 62 collected poems, 2014-2015/Sherna Spencer
>p.cm
>Includes index
>ISBN 978-0-9787613-3-2   (paperback)
>ISBN 978-0-9787613-4-9   (ebook/Kindle & Mobi)
>ISBN 978-0-9787613-5-6   (epub)

1. Caribbean. 2. Poetry. Women writers. 3. Inspirational-Women. 4. Humor -Women. 5.Title-

Library of Congress Control number 2015913120

First Edition: April 2016   SCANNABLE

>Printed in the United States of America

>Attention Corporations, Universities, Colleges and Professional Organizations. Quantity Discounts are available on bulk purchases of this book for educational, gift purposes, or as premiums for increasing magazine subscriptions or renewals.

>Special books or book excerpts can also be created to fit specific needs. For Information, please contact SGS Publishing, 4500 W. Oakland Park Boulevard, Ste 103 Fort Lauderdale, FL 33313: 954-714-8123.

Dedication:

For Uncle Lloyd and Iva Young who taught me a thing or two about life.

For all my other big sisters and brothers who are filling in the gaps.

Acknowledgements:

The author wishes to express her gratitude to her editors: Professor Rita Dorn, Beresford Nicholson and Kayla Bernal.

Contents

First Echo

Dancing	23
Happy Is	24

My BEginnING

Cross Multiply	29
Homesick	30
A Way...	31
Queen Tilde	33
Seeds for Planting	36

Love Notes

I'm in, Love	41
Love's All or Nothing	43
Love Sounds	45
One Love	46

Second Echo

Life's styles

Comfort and Convenience	49
Dust to Dust	50
Jammin' On	51
Life is...	52
Life's Rules	53
MAS	55

Mentoring from the Middle	56
Nick of time	57
The Wanderer	58

Mood swings

Old Time Religion	63
Only US	66
Pen In Hand	70
Set Free	72
Soul Speaking	75
Self	77
Ten Touches	78
The Whys Have It	81
Word Impact	82

Social Talk

Conquerors	87
The Deluded	88
Holiday Vow(el)s	89
I Am a Butterfly	92
Insulin in the MElaniN	93
Margarita Cano's World of Women	95
Meta	97
NoMad	98
Superfluous	99
The Alphabet Crossing Borders	100

Weighing In Lightly

Bare Instinct	105
Cringe & Brake	106
I'm In The Guinness	107
JapanJapan	108
Labels — Read Me!	110
Mom's Wow	112
Santa's Passovers	113

Third Echo

In the Moment

Miami Thrice	117
Once a Man	119
Physical Restraint	121

I Ode You

Cool Cat	125
He Knows You	129
Dill	121
Lost	133
Mandela's Slow Cooking	134
Maya, Queen Majesty	135
Night Sweats at WLRN	137
One Week At The Disco	140
Shelly Ann	143
Somebody's Child	144
Turns	146
War	147

TABLE OF CONTENTS STORY
TOCstory™

ShellyAnn, remember, He knows You Are Somebody's Child. Even though there are Wars, life's twists and Turns that gives us Night Sweats, He Knows you, Queen. By the way don't forget that Cool Cat is expecting you to bring some Dill to add to his Slow Cooking dish. After we eat we can go out to the Disco tonight, because it is a Holiday. I'm glad I found you in the Nick of Time. You were Lost, Free and Wandering Around, without any Comfort or Convenience somewhere in Margarita Cano's World of Women. I am speaking to you Soul to Soul, Mentoring you from the Middle, Planting Seeds: Why do you have to be pushover, like Santa's Passover? Don't Delude yourself, you are more than your Conquerors. You are not just Superfluous, having a Bare Instinct. You are more than just Meta. There is A Way to Love and Happiness. And with Pen in Hand, you will have Word Impacts and Cross MULTIPLY according to Life's Rules. You are a Butterfly, not a NOMAD, even though you don't like Labels. Once a Man said to me, Life is Jammin' on. I wonder, though, Why do we have to go back to the Dust. I know that Only US, ourselves can explain the How and the Why of the Insulin in the Melanin. Maybe they'll put us in the Guinness when we find out. It made someone Cringe because of the Ten Touches on the Brakes, on the way to Japan. You know over there Mom's Wow as they took the Alphabet with them as they Crossed the Border. We met them when they came to Miami Thrice, Once with a Man and the next time was with a Queen, named Maya, who explained Why she had come. I'm in Love, she said, I have met my One Love, I'm All In – it is the kind of Love that is All or Nothing. Sounds like real love to me. Give me that Old Time Religion and no Physical Restraint when we do MÁS Dancing, satisfying our inner Self, because we are Homesick.

First Echo

Dancing

I am a girl who loves to dance
I am so happy that sometimes I get a chance
I am so happy, I danced to France
I will never stop dancing,
'cause dancing
is my favorite thing to do,
with you.

Sonnet Spencer-Archer

Happy Is

Happy is hands clapping
snapping, waving in the air
foot stomping, blissful spinning with eyes closed.

Happy is keeping time
with the tap, tap, tap of your fingers on your right leg
a half-smile you aren't aware of gracing your lips.

Happy is your body moving
in unrehearsed choreography to the infectious bass line
as you watch yourself in your bedroom mirror.

Happy is staring so hard
at the canvas that you can see the brush strokes.

Happy is taking in the beauty around you
using all of your senses.

Happy is the sound of your loved ones' laughter.
Happy is defining yourself.

Happy is you at midnight
alone in the dark with the sound of your heartbeat,
beating in your ears.

Happy lives in the moments when your mind is furthest away
and your heart is closest.

Happy is your heart guiding you.

Suntia Spencer-Archer

My BEginnING

Cross Multiply

Seeds
seedlings
ripened fruit
leaves
bark
sunlight and rain
join together
to produce
more bounty.

Seeds from the Caribbean square
some flung,
others
drifted
away.

Homesick

Taking you in
my senses are attuned.
Sight, hearing, taste and smell
reacting,
when eager fingers
rip open the skin
of the ripe
burgeoning
orange
tangerine.

Heat trapped the smell of
diesel
sea salt
asphalt
familiar spices
the dry smoke from fields of burnt sugarcane.
Birds call
City traffic snarls.
I want to cuddle
and never leave.

A Way...

She had a way about her.
In the 1970's she was
hip with her hats,
broad with her baskets,
fashionable with stylish cotton
and sometimes
corseted dresses.
Gliding by with the queen-walk,
tall, head held high

She had a way about her.
Loving, with a welcoming persona,
a voice that carried a slightly haughty,
but inviting hello
or gave directives masked in a question,
"You wouldn't want
to do that, dear, would you?"
We wanted more

She had a way about her.
A generous, giving heart
whose blessings sprang from deep withIN
A soul with a life source that radiated
out to everyone around her.
A presence, an indescribable standout-ness
as though she was infused at birth

Three Echoes Dancing

with royal blood

She had a way about her.
A guardian of something,
something irresistible
and incandescent,
a treasure trove withIN.
A way about her, that is,
a Caribbean woman!

Queen Tilde~

~ Thy name is Tilde.
In the Spanish language,
you are used to accentuating the letter
over which you sit,
giving it emphasis, fattening its appearance,
deepening its impact.
Without your presence,
each letter would stand together with their other brethren,
in a **team**
dependent on each other
to make a word, a sentence or a paragraph,
or to give the meaning that the writer intended
or to be easy to recall, memorable.
You the Queen, is the milk in the café,
the spice in the *arroz con pollo.*
Everything you adorn becomes a stand out.

In the English language
your role, your purpose
is similarly large,
You're in charge.
You step alongside us with our every move,
defining the passage of time.
Not like clock-time that is exact,

Three Echoes Dancing

-in clock-time, you see a definite hour, minute or
second,
6:05:21 AM (wake up, its five minutes and 21 seconds
after six).
Clock-time is precise, it either is or it isn't,
like being pregnant, there's no in between.
In clock time, after a fleeting second
it is no more, that time has passed into the past.
Your *tilde* time is none of those
your *tilde* time is a stalwart
spanning decades!

Sitting on your English throne,
you explain the time from birth to death – the life-span.
Your curvy loop starts at a point, rises and forms the
crown
of a head turned sideways.
It then flows gently into a valley
before arching upward
ending on a mountain top
Suspended.

Your mark is unique, remarkable
the date of birth, written to your left,
is balanced by the date of death on the right.
You lie in between.
You are the queen,
the heart,

My BEginnING

the vibration,
the footprint and
the imprint.
You represent the life of that grandmother, grandfather,
mother, father, brother, sister,
niece, nephew,
cousin, child,
or grandchild.
You represent chef, teacher, preacher, flower arranger,
watch or bread maker, engineer or news reporter.
You are the source,
the Queen Bee.

~ Queen, you live your life
vicariously through and in us all,
through our lives' highs and lows,
through our sorrows, hopes and dreams.
Your accent is always in service;
new letters await your anointing.

In remembrance of Mrs. Iva Young, a wife, mother, big sister, friend, teacher, someone who was graceful, gracious, with a sense of humor and a giving heart.

Seeds for Planting

Your deeds send
seeds or
weeds
into the stratosphere.
An angel
tabulates them
and returns the list to you
for confirmation.

When the time came
for their review,
some railed,
throwing fits,
seeing
a life tied together
with
weeds.

Spill buckets
of seeds
across the billowy clouds.
They will return to you
as raindrops,
dancing to the ground
on a light breeze
welcomed

ready for planting,
anew.

Many Blessings to you as you plant the seed today that you want to reap tomorrow!

Love Notes

I'm in, Love

Rejoice, here comes the sun
stand
lean in
be infused
with the warmth,
the wisdom,
coming through
from ages past.
Bask in it,
let it be
the stage you're in.

Let the invisible rays
sink in,
creating a craze
a heavenly haze
to your gaze.
Don't let it be
only a phase.

Surrender to the warm infusion
Let it cling like a contusion.
Spread the patina,
push it to another.
Lean together

Three Echoes Dancing

like magnets attracting
and reacting.

Declare love as the
guide, the magnet, the metal,
pushing and pulling
directing our path
or it will be
the Grapes of Wrath.
Don't give in to any
other measure;
this is our only treasure.
Trade it.

Yes,
trade it,
for more.
I'm in,
you, love?

LOVE's All or Nothing

Love is the fire
blazing through the
arteries and capillaries
rampaging,
scorching,
every cell.

Love is the wind
creeping, silently approaching...
then pushing through the chest,
the lungs, the mouth,
exploding into the air,
"I love you."

Love is the rain
falling pitter, patter
drenching parched lips
pouring its liquid
on thirsty bodies,
cascading frenziedly.

Love is the sun
coating your pores
evenly,
one brush stroke at a time
with warm
yellow butter.

Three Echoes Dancing

Love is the moon
staring fixedly
in your face,
its smile
ear to ear,
an indulgent caress.

Love is the star
winking, twinkling,
alighting
on each strand of hair,
bringing it
to aching attention.

Love is a cloud
dense as cotton candy,
yet elastic, like a weighty balloon
whose bottom sags
and spreads
when filled with water.

Love is the sky
infinite, open
no eye can capture its vast reach.
Only love can mimic its limits.

Love's all in,
all or nothing.

Love Sounds

I know what happiness sounds like.
High pitched,
full of energy
that is exposed,
raw.
It is the mirror of love
when both of you are standing face to face.

One Love

Educate
elucidate
elevate
emancipate
liberate
yourself.

Congregate
meditate
mediate
create
illuminate
(t)each one.

Analyze
prophesize
don't polarize
don't demonize
all arise,
together.

One love
brimming
in the first Inning,
at last, winning
hear the rush
and feel the flush.

Second Echo

Life's Styles

Comfort and Convenience

Comfort is walking home in the night
cloaked in darkness
before the dew falls,
with your feet poured
toe to heel and
side to side
in firm soft leather,
all the while hoping gems of truth
will surface.

Comfort is listening and waiting
for inspiration from a star
your heart pumps at a slow crawl,
above the crackle
of your shoe
crushing a dry leaf,
and the tweets of the night flies
too, journeying home.

Convenience is not having to stop
to adjust your soles.

Dust to Dust

I walked in
drunk
with tiredness and desolation
after a day of job hunting.
Succumbing,
my body buckled
and collapsed.

I was like a hot air balloon
whose strength
dissipated with the release of the air
(its pent up life blood),
and became part of the surrounding earth's core.

Jammin' On

Electric guitars
at home with caviar and Renoir.
Boots worn by guys in
zoot suits
playing flutes
strummin'chords
stopping wars
with the beat
in the heat
in the streets;
and between the sheets.

Hot strings
at home with
wings and things.
Guys grooving and rocking with
fast palms, nimble fingers
and languid eyes
considered wise.
They beheld a beauty,
an island cutie.
The world needs this
eclectic booty.

Life Is...

Self-discovery comes about through
isolation and
introspection.

~

The world is made up of
pontificators, prognosticators,
humanists and hooligans.

~

Keep preaching to the (un)converted.
They can always benefit
from another tellin'.

Life's Rules: It *is* what it *is*

Juxtapose
just suppose
you knew
earlier,
that
the spice and the sauce
the ups and downs
is life

Juxtapose
just suppose
you knew
earlier,
that
the peanut brittle, coconut drops,
ice cream and crème brûlée desert
is life

Juxtapose
just suppose
you knew
earlier,
that
tulips and tourniquets,
bullies, bangles, beads and broaches
is life

Three Echoes Dancing

Juxtapose
just suppose
you knew
earlier,
that
minerals and funerals,
liars, laggards and lovers
is life

The labyrinth
of life
keeps us
walking
on air
seeking to be whole.

MÁS

I need
to be
who I am,
a*Live.*

To fit
into me,
the fire and light
the bright
inextinguishable
having foresight
me.

Hear the sound,
the vocal chord
of the arisen.
Feel the stub
of the birth chord
released.
See.
Taste.
Smell.
All's well.
I am
MÁS.
*M*y *A*uthentic *S*elf,
me.
Live.

Mentoring From the Middle

I want to be mentored so I can mentor you.
I want to be the best in-betweener, around on the ground, on your life's journey.
I wait to sit at the feet of the prophet, learning, growing bottom to top, top to bottom.
All of the wisdom to shorten my assent, to sharpen my comment. To go from simplistic assertions brought on by my age, mental orientation, condition and relationships.

My aim is to learn, to internalize, to experience, to be a bridge, a way for FOR(ward) you to test the waters with a bit of forewarning, a kind of hindsight, preventing a blindsight,
so you and I will learn to creep, to walk, to fly.

Nick of Time

I went through the amber light
and got there on time
in the nick of time.

I was spared an accident.
I was spared
to be a witness to your ups and downs
to be the storyteller of your life's trails and trials
to be your provider and your advocate
to bring you joy
in the nick of time, I was spared
to be
the me
that
I
wanted
to
be

In the nick of time
love found me

The Wanderer

I lost my way somewhere between birth and age 14

Maybe I toddled off
and they had to scatter
in all directions to find
me
and there were
no breadcrumbs,
for my curious soul
to follow
home

Maybe it was on the day I walked too far
in the sun looking for the peacocks
and when I found them, I waited too long
for them to acknowledge me
and then they did,
enfolding me in their plumes
the spectacle of colors: gold, purple, blue, red...
blinded me

Maybe it was my constant obsession with rainbows
I looked too long into their color lines,
drank too much of their fog,
as I tried to decipher how the colors came to be
and what made them depart

The explanation, "the devil and his wife are fighting
is why the sun and rain form the rainbow."
Who believes that, except young children searching for a reason?

Maybe it was the night we were listening to
stories of olden days, from Mr. Headly Mulgrave's
active imagination or keen recollection;
maybe who I was
met
with who I am
and decided to stay

Maybe after age 13 when I boarded the flight
and rode the wind,
it whispered in my ear and
I am still clogged.

Mood Swings

Old Time Religion

The world is on steroids
a meteor advancing.
To where
to what
in haste, are we dancing?
Could it be to a crash landing?
I'll share this with you
pass it along, do.
Right now
I just don't care
you hear?

Everyone is in a tizzy
telling you, "I'm busy"
"I'm dealing with my issue. Give me a tissue."
See them on TV, they've got drama, bad karma.
Meet them in the street
they're in heat.
They've got attitude.
I want to tell them
take a little latitude
an adjustment of the mood
and while you're at it, pass it on to your brood.

Three Echoes Dancing

Read what they write,
they're combative.
I want to give them a laxative.
They all say "I'm OK, you're OK."
They mean,
just stay away.
I am tired of this race to the top,
or is it to the bottom?
I am just tired...
tired of that rat race in my face.

Give me some old time religion,
going bird watching or
to movies.
Eating buttered popcorn and
cakes with drinks made by a show(er) of hands,
that adds love as an extra ingredient.
Add that fact to the label,
those are the foods I want on my table.

Give me that old time religion
making kites at Easter
sorrel at Christmas
crocheting
taking apart grandma's transistor radio
even watching corn grow.
Just taking it slow(er).

Mood Swings

Life's kinetic, running frenetic,
too hectic
makes us a heretic
from which the world
does not benefit.
For today, can I just lay back on the verandah
play cards, dominoes,
or jacks
and eat bammy and sprats?
That's good enough for me.
Yea, that's good enough for me today.

ONLY US (There is something In US)

I

There is only US.
The chicken and the egg syndrome acknowledged.
Life on earth means
everything begins and ends
with US

We know nothing but US.
We search for US,
for signs of who we are
where we came from
where we are going.
We search for understanding,
for the reason
we are here.

We are moving like hamsters on a treadmill
taking the next step.
Step after step
we move forward
not knowing
that we are moving on a circular road
around which we cannot see,
that we are not moving at all
but standing in place, shouting to the other side
trying to see

Mood Swings

and aching to know
US

II

Divine inspiration made us.
A divinity holds us hostage
in the world,
a gilded cage,
filled with all of our wants and needs?
Filled with good and bad
yin and yang
beautiful and ugly
sweet and salty.
Making compulsory roommates of US all.

We are standing in this round room
with a circular view,
not knowing
that we are standing in place,
shouting to the other side
trying to see
and aching to know
US

III

We build, we plant, we reap, we eat,
founding a Renaissance,
we believe.

Three Echoes Dancing

We conquered the darkness with halogen lights
tamed the animals; we here, you there
carved up the land with bricks and barriers
put speed to our feet with motorized engines
and dismissed the elements with a touch:
Cold to warm.
Warm to cool

We aim to seize control
of the earth
and sky,
trying to find the secret
to great unknowns in the universe.
We push, pull
slice, dice
carve, massage
seeking to make all that we know
conform to our ever increasing likes and dislikes.

We are standing on the edge of the earth,
Having a circular view,
not knowing
that we are standing in place,
shouting to the other side
trying to see
and aching to know
US

Mood Swings

IV

The atoms, arteries, capillaries,
the genes, the
oxygen
carbon
hydrogen
nitrogen
calcium
phosphorus
that makes US
is our BRAin trust.
It's a rocket thrust,
telling us to push on,
to conquer what we do not know.

The BRAsh in our braIN
has US moving
around
but like Surround Sound,
we are standing in place,
shouting to the other side
trying to see,
and aching to know
US

Pen In Hand

The mind's thoughts are reflected
in the eye,
the mind's eye.
The mouth is its orator,
the pen, its imprint.

It is said that the pen
is mightier than the sword.
Is the pen mightier
than the knife, the gun,
the bomb, the submarine?

Can words prevent an act
that causes the sword to fall
the knife to drop
the gun to retract
the bomb to expire
the submarine to reverse?

If the pen has might,
if the pen is right,
its words will not be slight.
It will be enough,
though the follow-through
might be rough.

Mood Swings

Let the mighty pen
ride the way
to a final act
that curbs self-interest,
that curbs greed,
that creates a new breed.

The mind can plant the seed
to trigger
mighty thoughts,
that both the mouth
and the pen
can deliver.

Set Free

I heard you.
It's not about the dog
that was hit by the car
that caused the tears to well up
and run.

It's the feeling that
inside
there is
an inescapable fire
that simmers,
invisible to all,
but whose
warmth is like an aura
around you
to which
no one dare
approach.

So the tear ducts
were released
from inside,
a dam overrun
with the force
from the weight in its belly.

Mood Swings

Without a sound,
it imploded,
blinding the eyes
blocking the nostrils
constricting the throat
cramping the neck
tightening the chest
buckling the legs
and feet

You breathed haltingly,
drawing in,
then expelled,
noisily,
pushing puffy eyelids apart.
The drops gripped
the tips of the eye lashes
but swift blinks forced them
to fall flat,
and presented a clear view
of the day.
Sunlight,
trees
sky
not a cloud high.

Stretch out your arms and hands
to capture the radiance

Three Echoes Dancing

the kiss, the warmth of life.
Unfold your legs,
stand
in the presence of
life to be lived.
Don't miss another day.
Take it,
make it your way.
You are
set free.

Soul Speaking

Your soul (mate) speaks of you
This is your life partner
the alter ego
conscience.
It is always at the ready
for a (tele) conference

Your soul is an invisible cloak.
It is caught hiding on your shoulders,
hunched as though dragging
an uncomfortably heavy weight or
upright, balancing on tiptoe,
graceful limbs on the verge of a spirited
purposeful move.
It is caught hiding in the eyes
in the clarity,
the cloudiness,
from the tears,
fears
and thoughts unspoken.

Your soul is alive.
It is the heat generated by thousands of
energy forces clashing together
combustible but not inflamed.
It adheres to its neighbors and attracts more,

Three Echoes Dancing

creating a zone of impenetrable air
you could not diffuse.

Your soul speaks for you.
answering all the questions about
who, what, when, where and why you are.
Listen.

Self

Self said to self
"Am I writing for you or for me?"
"Am I wide awake or asleep in a dream?"
I use this pen to capture and explain
the who, what, where, when, why or how
about myself, yourself,
my life and your life.

Am I awake or am I dreaming,
conjuring up situations,
living out the day's
unresolved or unrealized
experiences?

So be it.
If I am dreaming
I will soon awaken and continue
to write
to capture
to explain
the who, what, where, when, why and how
about myself, yourself,
my life and your life.

I will soon awaken
to face
myself.

Ten Touches

Ten touches wrings out the wet washcloth
and wipes your face.
Ten touches holds your belt firm
at the juncture of your back and spine,
stabilizing you as you start to wobble.
Ten touches adorns you in your Sunday best
giving you that needed zest,
if you're honest.

Ten touches lies side by side
enveloping the newborn in a cocoon
designed to replicate the womb.
Ten touches smoothes the bed sheets, the blanket,
the bed spread.
Ten touches is galvanized,
team-spirited,
to move across the body in tandem,
applying the right amount of pressure
to points of healing and pleasure.

Ten touches lifts the dirt and presses inside fruitful
grains
which are later reaped for our bodies' gains.
Ten touches are renegades with affinity
chopping, dicing, slicing all that is in their vicinity,
be it flesh or foul, fruit, spice or drinks,

Mood Swings

...then throwing in the ice.

Ten touches provides an imprint on paper evidenced by
coal black ink,
on cloth with bloody pinpricks from needles without
thimbles,
on vinyl records, 45 and 87 rpm's, that took heat in the
streets.
Ten touches squeezes sweetness from cymbals and
rumba boxes,
drums, guitars, trumpets, the trombone.
They can't be home alone, with the saxophone.

Ten touches devoured the flour, salt, sugar and butter,
yielding outcomes of confectionaries and pies
of guava, cream cheese, meat and potatoes.
Ten touches of tips following lips, eyebrows, jaw line.
Done!

Ten touches at the wheel of the car, boat, plane and
train--
bringing fame, fortune and fun in the sun
and with names like Wayne, Dwayne, Gloria and Sephoria
in Florida.

The mind calls, the tens answer,
their work is constrained only by our imagination
Our hands have seen the glory,

Three Echoes Dancing

the wonders of life
though the power of the ten fingers
that makes the hand,
that makes the impression that lingers,
that makes work light.

This poem was written as a tribute to the American workers in South Florida as part of the Smithsonian exhibit, <u>The Way We Worked</u>.

The Whys Have It

Question: Why do I have to...?
Answer: Getting from here
to there
means
moving,
leaving behind
a comfortable
existence

~

Question: Why did I do...?
Answer: The only way to know if you made the right
decision,
is to reflect.
Reflect upon what you learned.
Learning
means finding the truth
behind your actions.
The action means more than the words.

~

Question: Why am I here...?
Answer: Justify your existence.
Make the world remember
your face.
Leave a trace
some place.

Three Echoes Dancing

Word Impact

Once you open your mouth to speak
you have made a decision to do something,
to
make
a change.

My father used to say,
"Word is wind,"
when people did not keep their word.
My father used to say
"**Act**ions speak
louder than words."

I.
Dad, I have learned that words do not merely
shift things in the wind
staining the surrounding air with
dark thoughts
or unfulfilled promises.

Words are a **pact**–
a promise, a decision, a heavy dense ball;
throw it, roll it,
exchange it by hand.
Look at it ricocheting
to the destination.

Mood Swings

See its intended
and unintended
receivers,
as they feel
the im**pact**

II.

Dad, I have learned that words do not just
shift things in the wind
staining the surrounding air with
dark thoughts
or unfulfilled promises.

They bark, they bite,
they cut and they pierce.
The invisible wounds
im**pact**
the soul.
They send a message to the body
which slumps,
which sighs.
The mind
questions
why.

Three Echoes Dancing

III.

Dad, I have learned that words do not only
shift things in the wind
staining the surrounding air with
dark thoughts
or unfulfilled promises

They vibrate, they sizzle,
They bop, they hop,
hurrying to a welcoming
destination,
thoughts of future relations,
a time to dance
or a chance romance.

Words are a promise,
a **pact** to **act**.

Social Talk

Conquerors

We are more than our conquerors.
Though whipped and demeaned,
we are a mighty army of like minds
gleaming like stars
lighting up the night,
bursting with a love,
burning with the hopes and dreams of life.

Those heavenly lights are
so bright,
the Milky Way cannot contain them.
We came from that light,
we will return to its sight,
full of aromatic splendor
basking in the radiance of love.

Inspired by Romans 8:37-39

The Deluded

The Deluded,
are those
with
delusions,
having
jumped

to

    CONclusions

No

    PROS there.

Holiday Vow(el)s

As we plan to celebrate the coming holiday season, I would like to share
with you some thoughts on how you can take advantage of the time and enjoy it fully.

First, we need to become children again.
We need to relearn the alphabet, especially the vowels AEIOU.

There is a song that was popular around 1983
Where the chorus went like this:
"A, E, AEIOU, U and some sometimes Y
A, E, AEIOU, U and sometimes Y
A, E, AEIOU...."
Look it up and rock to the beat.
Have a little holiday dance.

We can sing and dance our way through the holiday season,
playing musical chairs together with our family,
singing just those 5 vowels.
How easy is that!
If you have forgotten how to play musical chairs,
ask a preschooler.
Soon you'll be dancing and having just as much fun as
when the Macarena and the Electric Slide came out.

Three Echoes Dancing

Next step.
Between November and February,
as our families and friends get together,
let's celebrate, by observing the
TOGETHER
part of that phrase.

Are you ready?
You have the vowels memorized and your family and friends are
TOGETHER?

This next step is BIG,
don't go off by yourself. Don't be
"ALONE TOGETHER."

If you are in a room of family and friends, but not
participating in the
celebrations because you need electricity
to communicate
because you are texting, talking, surfing....
(you know where I am going with this.)

Shut
iT
Off
Please

Social Talk

One last thing.
Sing or hum while you are shutting down
Apples
E's (mails, vites)
I's (pods, pads, phones) the
Out boxes, inboxes and sent message boxes and
Unknown senders, trapped in your spam box

Let's try this again,
"A, E, AEIOU
A, E, AEIOU"

I guarantee that doing this exercise will create
something
among you, your family and your friends,
that you will love.
It will create something that you can hold onto
beyond the holiday season,
something...
Totally
Open,
Glorious
Enticing
Totally
Happy
Eve**R**lasting

Three Echoes Dancing

I Am a Butterfly

I am a butterfly, not a moth.
I am a brightly colored stand-out.
My strength
is my persistence,
flying into and against the wind,
going one to one
giving,
like a bee pollinating.

Who sees the frailty
in bold wings
propelled by the heart,
the quiver of life
relentlessly,
pushing
forward?

Who sees the engine,
the fuel in the wings held together
by veins of thin thread
waxed for strength by the Maker,
soft to the touch,
free to fly
sky high?

Insulin in the MElaniN

Insulin
asserting
teaching
empowering
I & I
by and by
thy name is love

Insulin
running vein to vein,
the dosage
directly penetrating
the umbilical cord
by faith, by air,
by Joseph, Mary and Jesus

Someone said,
"The insulin is loose.
It needs a noose."
Collar it with
organization
streamlining regulations
standardization
harmonization
lockstep walkers, talkers, enforcers
inside and at the borders

Three Echoes Dancing

Insulin
squeezed out.
The puncture
to the vein.
Held hostage by hands
Fingers and gloves.
Rubber stretched
to show it,
to bring it to light.
Look carefully, you will see
the insulin disappearing,
getting soft,
getting flat
flat lining
flat lining

Boom boom, boom boom, boom boom
Wake up!
Call on
Joseph
Mary
Jesus

Bring back the insulin
the knowledge
the pride
the power.
The insulin in the MElaniN,
Thy name is love!

Margrita Cano's World of Women

Do their statuesque pose
and camera-ready stare
belie muffled,
wrenching
and absorbing
cries
from their silenced
souls?

Are their pent up
daydreams
and longings
caged behind
both natural and color painted lips,
socially and appropriately
depicted
by decree?

Are the fulsome cheeks and
vacuous eyes
girding the joy,
the enthusiasm
the exhilaration
the exclamation
the essence and soul
of the woman?

Three Echoes Dancing

They are surely not
a 21st century woman,
whose wants
and needs
are
fully
unbound.

Meta

Meta me
Meta you.
Let us share
now
not
LATA,
our
MetaDATA.

It's
critical
before
we
share
our
MetaPHYSICAL

Three Echoes Dancing

nomad nomad nomad nomad nomad

NoMad

Unending

Upending

Condescending

Know **I**t
All
(**NO** to)

it's just **MaD**dening

nomad nomad nomad nomad nomad

(border of "nomad" repeated vertically on both sides)

Superfluous

They're superfluous!

Parents and
Parenting,
Shared values.
Siblings
Rituals
Relatives
Friends and
Frenemies…

Who's left?
US.

Whatever,
who needs them,
we've got
Google

Three Echoes Dancing

The Alphabet Crossing Borders

OUTSIDE the USA, it's

Mr.
Mister!
Señor
Sir
Monsieur
Brother
Father
Vicar
Doctor
Barrister
Attorney
Elder . . .

INSIDE the USA, it's

Accused
Bad
Black
Brown
Colored
Criminal
Fearless
Fearful

Lazy
Shiftless
Suspect
Strong
*Un*broken
*Un*trustworthy
*Un*reliable
*Un*desirable
*Un*stable
*Un*wanted
*Un*necessary
Violent
Victim
H*un*ted
Ha*un*ted
Druggist (smuggler, taker).
Defenseless
Deadly

Weighing In Lightly

Bare Instinct

The mind talks
The body moves
1,2

You can train your mind, tell it what to do,
"Mind, tell my finger to point,"
or
"Mind, tell my throat to open
so I can swallow."
Done

What do you do if it does not want to?

Cringe & Brake

You wonder if you made a mistake,
but now you've realized, it's too late.

Your stomach tightens,
your hands curl into a ball
as you careen towards the wall.
Your feet push violently
into the floor.
You want to open the door.

You bark loudly,
"STOP!"

No you are not being squeezed by
a boa constrictor
you are taking a vow,
to hire a driving instructor.

I'm In The Guinness

Pardon me for shrinking
that violet is sinking.
I grew up with
prudence and pride,
everything we had to hide.

Privacy was the rule
now that's old school.
Everything was taboo
you have no clue.

Now playing catch-up
though at times I erupt--
that's MY private business!
So they put me
in the Guinness World Record, Under

"Last one to adapt to change."

Three Echoes Dancing

JapanJapan

I love the hibachi
the taste of the ginger,
the soy and salt.

The spices call out to me
all the time, as I drive past.
I shake my head and answer them
with an internal "No!"
You can't have me today Sir Spice,
even though you're nice.

But as I continue my ride,
my thoughts slide.
I can imagine,
the chef preparing,
their dexterity is their brevity,
throwing containers high in the air
with a flair.

They deftly catch the cans before
sprinkling the horde of spices
from on high
and them leave them to their own devices,
to descend gracefully
to a waiting tableau.

In The Moment

Oh, what a sight to be seen.
The spices atop vegetables and meat
pursed with steam.

They join their brethren
who have already contributed
their granule bites
for our
gastronomical delight!

Labels
Read Me!

I like them and yet I don't.
They're either too confining or
they shout at me.

I want to discover their meaning accidentally
or unravel the puzzle,
challenging myself to figure out
what I want to believe or
what I want to throw out.

Then I saw in a magazine an interesting name
"Peanut-Crusted Tofu Tacos with Tangy Slaw."
"Wow," I thought, "is that a cross between a
Southerner
A vegan, (Ok the person could be from anywhere)
A Mexican and
A European (probably a German or Polish native)?
You might need all of that mix
in your gene pool to enjoy that combination!"

My curiosity kept me reading the list of ingredients.
Low and behold!
The recipe called for
coconut milk
peanuts

In The Moment

breadcrumbs
eggs
cabbage
pepper
scallions
lime juice
and of course, tofu and tortillas.

I did not take a blood test or a "guesstimate"
about whether or not I would enjoy this motley mix.
Eyes saw, brain read, genes screamed,
Coconut! Peanuts! Pepper! Scallions!
Read me!
Feed me!

Mom's Wow

Mom's pickup the slack,
where you can't see;
committed to helping you to be

You might say she is a dragon
or that she is out of fashion

Tempest, storms and tears will fly
your (im)patience will reach the sky

Through it all, faith is the driver.
Hear her pray
God please deliver

Santa's Passovers

Santa will not stop at our house this year.
Our children
were caught short,
being naughty,
not nice.

The children, in their haste
when taking out the waste
left open the top
causing the trash to drop
and fly into the neighbor's lawn,
creating a trashy storm.

The neighbors in their grief
called the police
to report
a breach,
of the
peace.

Our children were floored, complaining,
a knock on the door
bringing it to our attention
would have prevented them
from suffering
from Santa's omission.

Three Echoes Dancing

By and by
they said they would try
to slow down
and not frown,
when the neighbors
are in town.

Third Echo

In the Moment

Miami Thrice

Ah, the 305.
The 786.954.754.561
The heat
The beat
The re-treat

Where visitors
and 'gators
lounge around
basking,
and former generals,
presidents and dictators,
barons
and their ladies
chill.
They're not here to shrill

Sometimes the hunters and the hunted
do a stare-down,
four eyes behind tinted glasses
across steamy streets.
They sit at marble and granite tables
with their rum punch, cigars,
café
and latte

Three Echoes Dancing

Behind them: actions,
pulpit, politics,
power
and might.
Big rims of hummers
double M's (Mercedes, Maseratis)
double R's (Rolls Royce)
bling and gin

Before them: reactions,
Dr. Scholls, Web MD,
Honda
and Accord.
After iced tea on the verandah,
some may wander.
Bedtime at dusk
becomes a must

It's all just par for the course
In the 305.
The 786.954.754.561
The heat
The beat
The re-treat

(Note: The 3 area codes are for Miami, Fort Lauderdale and Palm Beach)

Once a Man

Our grandparents said
"Once a man, twice a child."
It's true, I now see it firsthand.
Heads in your face
inspecting eyes,
skin, hair and nails.
None observe your personal space.
Privacy is not a word
that can be heard.

Hands touching, massaging,
wiping your skin and body,
directing its movements.
The nerve endings and muscles take you about
in a jerky gait or
keep you grounded,
lying prone.
Sometimes you are wheelchair-bound,
pushed around.

Voices rise above yours,
words drone out your thoughts and wishes
it's like you're caught in a net with other fishes.
You reluctantly comply,
even as your will
blazes

Three Echoes Dancing

like a fire igniting,
and
diffusing rapidly.
Your desire is truncated,
leaving uncomfortable
contemplation
until the next thought arises.

Physical Restraint

Don't let me stare at the ceiling;
There is nothing left there to ponder.
Let me see the Hibiscus, Bougainvillea,
pink and red in glorious bounty
or
the singularly outstanding
ginger and anthurium
in their own skins.

Place them on my table,
along with a piece of mango,
and a few pegs of tangerine.
Right there, yes.
Right next to my teacup,
warm with my mint.
Let the table be amidst
lush surroundings,
in a cornucopia of texture and depth.
Set it in warm earth tones,
vibrant color patterns
of cotton, silk, and satin.
Ditch the placid,
or rather the standard
cookie-cutter white
to which I have never adhered.

Three Echoes Dancing

Let me smell the fresh air mixed with scents of cooking.
Let me hear the *labrish* of the cooks
as they make the pots dance to the rhythm of their hands.

Let the walls and halls vibrate energetically,
but hold firm onto the output
of musicians collaborating with the bass and drums.
Let me hear them laying on the life force
from their kinetic instruments.

Let me imagine taut bodies of the young as they,
with brows knit in concentrated effort,
open their thorax to expel their sound:
the new voice of the day.
Let me see their cells distended, straining,
bursting to be the best they can be,
being how I remember,
being me.

Cool Cat

He was a cool cat,
a good looking man.
There was always a hat or a tam,
perched jauntily on his head.
Dapper and a great dresser,
he loved shoes, a well-cut pair of pants and cologne.
You could always pick up a bottle of something
and he was appreciative.
He didn't ask for much.

Somewhere around 1974, he took us on a ride
to Blackstone Edge, St. Ann.
Photos were taken both before we left
and at our destination.
There he was,
in his banlon shirt and well-pressed pants,
leaning on his yellow Volvo, with that smile,
confident, indulgent as though he was smiling
with you.

Friendly and accommodating,
Mr. Cool Cat made friends easily.
He was a down-to-earth person,
naturally easy-going.
Just play some Alton Ellis, John Holt
or Freddy McGregor

Three Echoes Dancing

and Cool Cat felt the
call to his brethren.

Mr. Cool Cat was a man of few words.
Any conversation would find him quietly taking it in
then...
Bam!
He would summarize the issue in one or two sentences,
and add a bit of wisdom.
And that was that!
My aunt would say, "after Lloyd talk, argument over."

Mr. Cool Cat, who nicknamed my daughter,
"Summer Bounce"
after she spent a memorable summer around him,
was a fan of the youth.
Flying feet would run to greet him whenever his car
was spotted purring down the driveway .
He always had a little something:
favorite snacks, sweets, coins and other bounty,
overflowed from the car seat to the trunk.
One day a find for my sister and me: our first pair of
gold earrings!

Cool Cat did not know how to say no.
If you asked him for something,
the next time you saw him,
he had the desired item,

I Ode You

or he would show up when he knew he would be needed
without you having to ask a second time.
He was unfrazzled, almost offhand,
he did not want a BIG thank you...
He knew he was our number one.

Over the years, we traveled the island with a posse
Lilly Bell,
Patsy, Wayne, Deniel, Cheri (whom he called "Cherry"),
Sunita and Sonnet.
Cool Cat drove us for over 5 decades,
without incident or accident.
We went to Port Royal, Bluefields, Nannytown,
the Blue Mountains,
Treasure Beach, Bath, Milk River, Little Ochi,
Montego Bay, and many more...

Most of the time there were three generations
in one car.
Mr. Cool Cat was tour guide.
He had been to the airport hundreds of times,
but never took a flight.

My favorite destination? Devon House I-Scream.
It was my preferred first stop after landing at the airport.
No worries about the scale and counting pounds.

Three Echoes Dancing

I will miss the food,
his cooking, the traveling,
the inspiring, quiet countenance
of the Cool Cat man known to some as "Socks."
For me, he was just my uncle.

Dedicated to my uncle, Lloyd Thompson, who passed away on March 4, 2014. In his early and later years, he lived his life according to how it was given to him; in the middle years, he lived life the way he chose and was who he wanted to be.

He Knows You

I never met you
I never will
but He did.

He knew you before you were a seed
He gave you life
He caused you to breathe.
He sent you on a mission
to provide for some a vision
and for others
to make them laugh, smile,
dance and cry
---He knows why.

At times you walked
in his shoes
he always walked
in yours.
He knew you more
than you knew yourself.
He knew you
He was you.

Now He has taken you back to Himself
you are needed for another task
I am sorry He did not ask.

Three Echoes Dancing

No one was prepared for you to leave
we find it hard to believe.
How could he make you so sickly
and take you so quickly?
We thought we owned you,
but He had just loaned you
to us
To make us laugh, smile,
dance and cry
He knows why.

It's our loss
but His gain,
despite the fact that we are in pain.

We cannot forget
your love and kindness
my brother.
He left your soul and spirit inside us
to guide us.

For Giselle and family on behalf of her brother.

Dill

Dill
A green vegetable with
Thin wisps that
belie its physical strength.
Tart to taste.
Like hot pepper,
to be eaten in small doses.

Directions to eat Dill:

    1. Bite.
        As the essence paints your whole mouth,
        the taste buds exclaim,
        "This is insane!"
        (Watch out, the back corners will get an
        extra share!)
    2. Breathe in sharply.
    3. Again!
    4. Taste with more confidence.
    5. Breathe in again.
    6. Chew.
    7. Swallow.
    8. Clear your palate.
    9. Repeat.

Laugh at and eat everything

Three Echoes Dancing

bitter and sweet,
LIVE !
it's life.

For Phyllis Diller

Lost

Where did you go?
If I need you where will I look?
Where are the crumbs, the trail that leads to you.?
In whose soul is yours intertwined?
You were too vibrant to have just melted into the stratosphere.

You must be close,
You would not want to wander too far away from us.
I want to see your eyes brighten when you are happy,
to hear your voice matter-of-factly declaring
your point of view.

I did not like to see you in pain;
you groaned with your eyes closed, with a sense of finality.
Then you stopped and just breathed, letting the pain have its way.
It won.
We lost.

I want to find you,
to know
where you are.
To keep you close.

Dedicated to Hugh Palmer, music engineer, whose favorite words were: "I am an engineer, not a mechanic."

Mandela's Slow Cooking

Bob Marley's "Exodus, movement of Jah people"
kept him going.
The Idea.
One Man.
Man
del
a.

Equality.
Sacrifice.
Truth.
Love.
Defiance.
All took
time.

Bondage.
The antidote to
apartheid:
Determination.
Tears.
Hope.
Dignity.
Won.

U.S. President Barack Obama said, "Never discount the difference that one person can make..."

Maya, Queen Majesty

Three score and ten
could not hold you.
The grace,
the majesty in the thought,
tone and speech,
heralded
you,
Lady Maya

I bow,
I lay prostrate
at your feet,
an apprentice,
hoping,
trusting
that your aura
would be contagious

I dedicate a song to you,
the legendary Curtis Mayfield's "Queen Majesty,"
for my words would seem
superfluous
amongst the millions
in awe of your
pure
splendity*

Three Echoes Dancing

We do not mourn.
Your gifts are your pledge
to spread love and peace.
We honor your message
and carry them in us.
You are with us.
We rise together.
We are one

Dedicated to Maya Angelou
*In your honor, I have created a new word that describes you: Splendity.

Splendity: [splen-di-tee]
(noun.) the essence of grace and lovingness

I Ode You

Night Sweats at WLRN

Tracy, I'm in Love.
Its 8:00 PM, and I hear your smooth voice announce,
"This is the real Tracy Fields."
Without fail, I think,
"There couldn't have been another who
dared to try
to duplicate your iconoclast sound!"
Your music is ripe
for toe tapping and lovemaking.
You hooked me,
a holdover from WHQT LOVE 94.
Its abrupt shutdown
left me 1/2 full

The night moves with trumpets,
violins, piano,
the sax.
Strident, vibrant,
full octaves of sound.
Leontyne Price,
pure gold on the train.
Night train.
Old time radios,
foxtrot, juke box,
wining and dining.
In other words,

Three Echoes Dancing

liming

Daytime hours
were filled with mind matters
and manners.
Ted Talks and Ophira,
let's ask her for another go-round with Car Talk;
it is a radio laboratory.
But wait, wait, Let's consider all things
like home companions, folks and acoustics too.
Even America's test kitchen.
Let's ask Tavis for a smiley, here and now,
and our message will surely reverberate around the
world,
starting with reams of Diane.

What say you?
You want a getaway, to get some fresh air in the
morning, maybe this weekend?
Why not just stay around and re-read the book
called, *On Being an Aristocrat*?
We might get information that is on the money,
so we do not have to make a snap judgment.
Although I wish it were only a game,
it is still a good topic for the tropics.

Night turns up again
in the 305.786.954.754,

I Ode You

The Bahamas and more.
25 years of night solstice with Clint O' and
then Rich, the man inside my radio.
Nights in arms, babies, bottles, milk,
Baileys and rum, Redstripe, Heineken, a babe,
a calypso corner, a waltz, a whine,
dub, rocksteady,
rent a tile.
Night tunes
we were local with Bob, not Dizzy,
Queen Ifrica and Marcia, not Etta
sweet nights
the baseline...
holding time with
rockers
sound-clash,
all on the A side.

Now all we have is the B side,
twice
and a C.

Psaaw.*

*unfortunately

One Week at the Disco

Donna
It was not a chance
you were the
Diva of the Disco Dance.
Let's
quantify your contribution
to the disco
revolution

Let's
dance the days and nights away
dress our best
grab a partner
hit the
runway to
feel the magic of those
disco days

Let's,
every day,
play,
your songs until they are done
then start again
with the first one
Let's play on
      Sunday – Heaven Knows

I Ode You

    Monday – She Works Hard For The Money
    Tuesday – Let's Dance
    Wednesday – On the Radio
    Thursday – Dim All the Lights
    Friday – Love to Love You Baby
    Saturday – Bad Girls

Then the radio dropped the ball
after playing only seven––
it was just eleven,
we were still on the floor
we weren't ready for the door

We called out to the DJ, "Let's go all the way
play more, the rest of her Billboard Top 20 score"
Let's hear
    No More Tears
    Hot Stuff
    McArthur Park
    The Wanderer
    I Feel Love
    This Time I Know It's For Real
    The Woman In Me
    Love Is In Control
    There Goes My Baby
    Cold Love
    Spring Affair
    Walk Away

Three Echoes Dancing

   I Love You.

Love to love you, Diva.
Let's not stop
the Disco.

Dedicated to Donna Summer

I Ode You

Shelly Ann

Socialite

Helpful

Electric

Loving

Large

Yeah

A **N**atural **N**ubian

Braata* for my friend

Strong
Humble
Elegant
Leader
Lively
Young

A**N**noi**N**ted

You are missed.

a little more or something extra

Three Echoes Dancing

Somebody's Child

(Some)body's child
    all are...

Somebody's child cried out
in vain
in pain,
both palpable,
and throbbing,
then
laid to rest.

Somebody's father
Somebody's grandfather
Somebody's grandson
Somebody's son
Somebody's nephew,
grand nephew
godfather.

Father God
rest their souls
that echo
ceaselessly,
restlessly,
in
the wind.

I Ode You

Persecutors:
give me a reason
to love you,
to "love my neighbor as myself"
for my heart aches.
My heart is breaking
for the children,
our children,
God's children.

Ah,
a flicker of (in)sight
Father God's in control.
We are but mortals
on the ground
we only have one go-around.
Where is the need for
combative expletives?
Time for reflections and new selections.

For Eric Garner and countless others, named and unknown. All are Somebody's children.

Turns

To everything there is a season.
Garlic, scallions, onions,
sometimes salt and pepper,
blended well.
Sometimes sour and sweet,
sour or sweet.
Sometimes cold, cool,
hot and back again.

To everything there is a reason.
Hail, thunder, sun, rain;
not in vain.
Moonlight, starry night, daylight
planting and reaping
laughing and giggling
sleeping
weeping.

Amazing grace
how sweet the sound
I saw.
I see.
Now I know Thee.

Dedicated to Pete Seeger

I Ode You

WAR

Steven J. Sotloff
James Foley
exposed pain and suffering,
where there was no accountability.
Perpetrators
control and
silence
the opposition.

Compensation is a western word.
Consolation from the world bodies,
who admit to being slow on the uptake
while many die in vain, in pain.
Perpetrators
control and
silence
the opposition

W
A
R

is

Why Angels Roar

ABOUT THE AUTHOR

Sherna Spencer's roots spring from the Island of Jamaica. Her love of books and language began there in a Parish library, in Manchester. After moving to the U.S., she attended Le Moyne College in upstate New York. There, she obtained a Bachelors degree, with dual majors in English and Spanish. She continued her studies in Italy and thereafter completed her law degree at the University of Miami School of Law. She is currently an attorney in Fort Lauderdale, Florida. For nine years, she was the host of a live radio program broadcast to listeners in South Florida and the Bahamas.